PHILIP DE JERSE

C000241717

CELTIC COINAGE IN BRITAIN

SHIRE ARCHAEOLOGY

Cover photograph
Coins of the Corieltauvi,
late first century BC and early first century AD.

British Library Cataloguing in Publication Data:
de Jersey, Philip
Celtic Coinage in Britain. - (Shire Archaeology; no. 72)
1. Coins, Celtic - Great Britain
I. Title
737.4'9361
ISBN 0 7478 0325 0

Published in 2001 by
SHIRE PUBLICATIONS LTD
Cromwell House, Church Street, Princes Risborough,
Buckinghamshire HP27 9AA, UK.
Website: www.shirebooks.co.uk

Series Editor: James Dyer

Number 72 in the Shire Archaeology series.

ISBN 0 7478 0325 0.

First published 1996; reprinted 2001.

Printed in Great Britain by CIT Printing Services Ltd, Press Buildings,
Merlins Bridge, Haverfordwest, Pembrokeshire SA61 1XF.

Contents

Acknowledgements

Many people have contributed enormously to my own understanding of British Celtic coinage, both through their published work and in conversation. I would particularly like to thank John Sills, S. W. Bragg, Geoff Cottam, David Holman, Jeffrey May, Amanda Chadburn, Simon Bean, Colin Haselgrove, Richard Hobbs, Andrew Burnett, Daphne Briggs, Chris Rudd and Bob Van Arsdell for generously sharing their knowledge with me. I am also grateful to S. W. Bragg and Daphne Briggs for their valuable comments on earlier drafts of this text.

An important aspect of a book such as this is its illustration, and I am grateful to Simon Pressey for drawing figure 4, to David Holman for supplying photographs of coins found in Kent, and to Jennie Lowe and Bob Wilkins for providing the bulk of the photographs from the records of the Celtic Coin Index.

Last, but by no means least, I would like to extend my thanks to all the people – collectors, dealers, archaeologists, museum curators and individual metal-detector users – who contribute details of coins to the Celtic Coin Index, without which our knowledge of the late iron age in Britain would be much the poorer.

List of illustrations

Note on illustrations

Unless otherwise stated, all photographs of coins are reproduced at twice actual size.

1
Coinage in Celtic society

Celtic coins provide the most common form of material evidence for life in Britain in the late iron age, from shortly before the Roman conquest of Gaul in the mid first century BC to the defeat of Boudicca in AD 61. During this period coinage in Britain developed and flourished in one of the most spectacular displays of artistic and technical innovation seen anywhere in the Celtic world. This book examines the main themes of this development, describing the coins and explaining how and why they were made, and what they can tell us about society at the end of the iron age.

Britain was the last part of the Celtic world to adopt coinage. On the continent the first Celtic coins were produced from the end of the fourth century BC, based on the gold stater of Philip II of Macedon, who ruled between 359 and 336 BC (figure 1). This coin weighed between 8.5 and 8.6 grams and was struck in gold of about 95 per cent purity. On the obverse is the wreathed head of Apollo, and on the reverse, above Philip's name, a two-wheeled chariot (*biga*) pulled by two prancing horses, driven by a charioteer holding a whip. This coin was issued not only by Philip, but also (and in greater numbers) by his successors, Alexander the Great, Philip III and Cassander, down to 294 BC.

1. Gold stater of Philip II of Macedon (above) and a Celtic imitation (below). (Institute of Archaeology, Oxford; David Holman.)

Each of these men employed huge numbers of Celtic mercenaries, and it was through their service in these Mediterranean armies that the Celts were first exposed to coinage on any significant scale. We cannot be certain how many staters they received for their service – perhaps just one for a season's employment – but it is clear that they took them back to their homelands

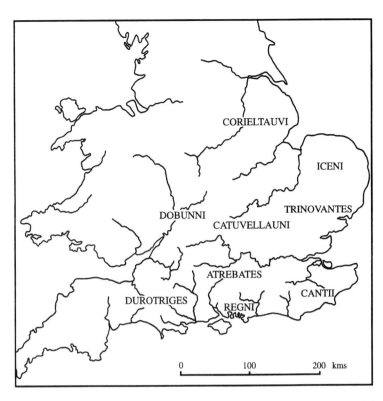

2. Coin-using tribes in iron age Britain. The two most powerful kingdoms were formed of the Trinovantes and Catuvellauni, to the north of the Thames, and the Atrebates and Regni to the south. Beyond these tribes of the south-eastern core lay the four peripheral coin producers, the Durotriges, Dobunni, Corieltauvi and Iceni.

and in some cases began to produce their own versions of the coin (figure 1). Thus began more than three centuries of coin production among the Celtic communities of Europe, eventually to include some of the island peoples on the north-west periphery of the continent.

The first significant developments in Britain were directly related to coinage produced in Gaul: firstly a series of imports from Belgica and central or southern Gaul (chapter 3), then a series of British imitations of these coins, produced in many different areas of the south and east of the country (chapter 4). The use of coinage in Britain was restricted almost entirely to the territory south-east of a line from the Severn to the Humber (figure 2). This territory can be conveniently divided into two zones, a core and a periphery. The core comprised the two most powerful late iron age kingdoms, to the north and south of the Thames (discussed in chapters 5 and 6), plus Kent, which for most of this period was controlled by one or other of these dominant kingdoms. From approximately the end of the first century BC the core tribes produced increasingly Romanised coinage, indicative not only of their geographical proximity to Roman Gaul, but also of the enthusiasm with which their leaders engaged in trade with the continent. Strabo (*Geography* IV, 5, 2) records that they exchanged 'grain, cattle, gold, silver and iron...also hides, and slaves, and dogs...suited to the purposes of the chase' for luxury goods, including wine and fine pottery. It may be argued that in becoming so accustomed to the availability of these goods the south-eastern tribes were prepared for invasion by Rome, a 'softening-up' process which had already usefully accompanied Rome's expansion through Gaul.

Around the core was a zone of peripheral tribes, mostly separated from the principal routes to the continent by the core (with which they exchanged goods), and generally much more resistant to the processes of Romanisation. These tribes maintained the characteristically Celtic designs of their coinage throughout the last century of their independence (chapters 7 and 8).

Although Celtic coinages in Britain are generally thought of as 'tribal' productions, this term is not always appropriate. The boundaries of the tribes named on figure 2 were not set down until the Roman period, and – particularly for the early uninscribed coinage – some types simply do not correspond well to the boundaries of a century or more later. In some cases it is therefore better to use simple geographical or neutral terminology, and this approach has been adopted here. There is a further, more complex problem with the concept of 'tribal' production, related to the structure of Celtic society, and we should briefly examine here what we know of the societies that produced the coins.

Julius Caesar wrote in *De Bello Gallico* (VI, 13-15), his account of the campaign to conquer Gaul, that there were two classes of people in the Celtic world: the free and powerful, comprising knights and druids; and the rest, who were little better than slaves. Although this emphasises the differences between the agricultural producers and the warrior nobles, the two groups had close social and economic ties, based principally on the system of clientage. In traditional Celtic society, a warrior noble would enter into formalised relationships with peasant farmers, allowing them to use his land or loaning them cattle, in return for which the farmers gave him a proportion of their produce. There were benefits to both sides: the noble had an interest in protecting his cattle and hence looking after the peasant farmer, while the farmer could also be called upon to provide military service. The more cattle at a noble's disposal, the more followers he could gain, and hence receive more produce; this could be dispensed at feasts, in public displays of largesse which were extraordinarily important in maintaining the social hierarchy.

The disadvantages of this system are not difficult to imagine. Warfare, at least on a relatively small scale, was endemic to the society, since the warrior could only enhance his prestige through raiding and looting. Temporary alliances might be formed between nobles, but they rarely persisted or developed to encompass large areas of territory with stable and centralised government.

The introduction of coinage into this society provided an ideal medium for nobles to make gifts and payments to their followers: it was convenient and could carry a design recognisable to all as a symbol of value and authority. Coinage at this stage was not used in everyday exchange or in regular trade with the outside world, but as one of a number of objects which anthropologists call 'primitive valuables' or 'primitive money', manufactured only sporadically as need arose; the quantities produced would have depended not only on need, but also on the resources – of bullion and of metalworkers – available to the issuing authority. Hence the appearance of localised issues such as the Cheriton stater (chapter 4) or the early uninscribed silver from southern Britain (chapter 5), which are almost certainly not tribal issues but the products of *pagi* – subdivisions of the tribal unit – or of minor and relatively transitory authorities.

During the last years of the first century BC and into the first century AD the nature of the Celtic societies in south-east Britain changed quite dramatically, primarily because of contact with Roman Gaul. Now the power and prestige of the warrior nobles rested less on their success in cattle-raiding and more on their ability to form advantageous alliances with the providers of luxury goods from across the Channel. For the first time the signatures of centralised mints appear on unquestionably tribal coinages, though it is still possible that at some periods lesser kings, or rulers of parts of a tribal territory, were able to strike their own coinages: for example the various names associated with Tasciovanus (chapter 6). Large numbers of relatively low-value coins, such as the commoner bronze issues of Cunobelin, are found on important settlements, where as well as being used for subsistence or service payments they may finally have performed a function not unlike our coinage today. Meanwhile the high-value gold staters continued to be produced and used only by the upper echelons of society, performing the traditional function of gift exchange between more or less important noble families, and thus still playing an important role in binding together the fabric of Celtic society on the eve of the Roman conquest.

The finer points of the subject of how the Celts used their coins are often controversial. We are still uncertain, for example, exactly how the early Kentish potin coinage (chapter 4) was used: as an unusually early example of a low-value coinage used on major settlements, or as a relatively high-value gift alongside the gold coinages of the period? These questions will be answered only through archaeological excavation, where the context of the coin is carefully recorded, rather than through metal-detector discoveries, which in other respects have provided enormous quantities of new information since the mid 1970s.

While aspects of their use may be problematic, we have a better idea of how Celtic coins were made. The processes of striking and casting used to manufacture British Celtic coinage will be discussed in the next chapter.

2
Techniques of manufacture

British Celtic coins were produced in two ways, conventionally described as struck and cast. The vast majority of coins were struck, the only phases of cast coinage occurring near the start of the British series in Kent (chapter 4) and at the end of the series in Dorset (chapter 7). Both methods required a considerable level of technical sophistication to ensure the successful production of coinage.

The process of striking a coin began with the production of a blank. It seems likely that in most cases a blank was formed in a clay mould (often known as a pellet mould or pellet tray; figure 3); many fragments of these moulds have been discovered on late iron age sites, notably more than three thousand pieces at Old Sleaford in Lincolnshire, in three sizes possibly corresponding to stater, silver unit and silver half-unit. Traces of gold, silver and copper have been detected in some moulds, indicating that they were certainly used for working precious metal, if not demonstrably for coinage. Opinion differs on exactly how the metal alloy was placed in the mould. It was almost certainly not poured in as molten metal, since this method would not allow the precise weight control evident in much Celtic coinage (see below). Instead the metal may have been put into the mould in powder or nugget form and then heated. Recent discoveries also suggest that metal ingots may have been very carefully divided into the appropriate weights and added to the pellet moulds.

An alternative technique may have been simply to pour a slug of molten alloy on to a flat surface, to be cooled and then struck (it has been suggested that this method was used for some continental issues) but this would have entailed problems of weight control similar to pouring molten metal into moulds.

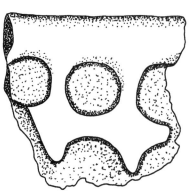 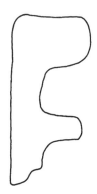

3. Clay pellet mould from Canterbury. The central hole is approximately 1 cm in diameter. (Based on *Kent Archaeological Review*, 1982, 163.)

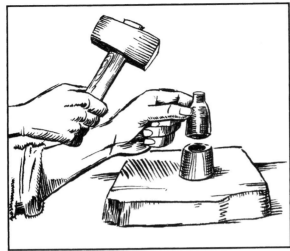

4. Possible technique for striking Celtic coins. (Simon Pressey.)

Once the metal had been heated in the mould it would normally have to be flattened before striking. The temperature at which this could be successfully achieved probably depended on the composition of the alloy. This also had implications for the actual striking process, since some alloys may have been too hard to be effectively struck cold. The flattened blanks, or *flans*, were struck by hand, placed on a concave obverse die – to hold the blank in place – and struck with the convex reverse die (figure 4). The dies themselves were made of iron and/or bronze. Very few Celtic dies survive and only part of the obverse die of a Gallo-Belgic stater, discovered in Hampshire, is recorded from Britain. Presumably they were closely guarded while they were in use, and many were used until destruction. For the early coinage in particular, the dies tended to be bigger than the area of the flan, in some cases as much as twice the width of the image on the coin, which consequently shows only a part of the design (figure 5).

The quality of engraving on many Celtic dies is superb. Some of the silver minims produced by the Atrebates are barely 7 mm in diameter, and within those 7 mm are beautifully detailed images such as the bust and horse on the uninscribed type shown in figure 6. The tools used to

5. The obverses of two Cheriton staters (British D). The design on the coin on the left is nearly central, while the coin on the right has been struck far off-centre but still does not show the edge of the design. (Institute of Archaeology, Oxford.)

engrave such tiny details have not yet been recovered, and we are still ignorant of many aspects of this process: the extent to which punches were used for repetitive decoration, for example, or the possibility that more than one person worked on different aspects of a single die. It is occasionally possible to detect the hand of the same die-cutter on different types of coinage; this has great potential in solving problems of typology and chronology.

6. Uninscribed silver minim of the Atrebates. The illustrations on the left are at actual size, those on the right at four times actual size. (Institute of Archaeology, Oxford.)

The artistic ability of the Celts was matched by their expertise at controlling the weight and the alloy of the coinage. Weights were controlled at the start of the process, when the nuggets or ingots of metal were added to the pellet moulds, or possibly when the blank was flattened, rather than through modification of the final coin. The moneyers were capable of producing many thousands of coins to within a small percentage of the intended weight: for example the normal face/horse silver units of the Iceni, deviating by just a few milligrams each side of 1.21 grams, or the later staters of Cunobelin, grouped even more tightly around 5.40 grams.

Such precise weight control also required a detailed knowledge of the composition of the alloy. The proportions of gold, silver and copper in the ternary alloys which made up the stater coinage were subtly altered during the course of British Celtic coinage, generally so that more coins could be struck from smaller amounts of precious metal. Over the century or so of development described here, the gold content of the main series of staters dropped from 70 per cent or more to approximately 40 per cent; the amounts of silver and copper correspondingly rose, the latter causing the characteristic reddish tinge of much of the later British Celtic coinage. It is possible that some of the decoration on the coinage includes privy marks which indicated the gold content to those who understood them; this is most likely to have been the case for some of Cunobelin's gold (figure 7), but too few analyses have yet been carried out to confirm this.

Comprehensive programmes of metal analysis are a relatively new development in the study of British Celtic coinage, but they have already both confirmed the skill of the moneyers and added valuable information

7. Gold stater of Cunobelin. The X above the MV may be a privy mark. (Institute of Archaeology, Oxford.)

on the composition of some alloys. So, for example, many Atrebatic silver units of the early first century AD (chapter 5) are virtually identical in composition to Roman Republican denarii, which probably provided the source material. Some bronze coins of Tasciovanus (chapter 6), struck at the start of the first century AD, are actually brass. They contain significant quantities of zinc in their alloy, which may have been imported in the form of Roman or Gaulish coinage, or as brass *fibulae* (brooches). Further studies will undoubtedly reveal more information on the sources of the metal and the processes of production.

Many, if not most, of the gold coinages and some silver types are also known in the form of contemporary plated forgeries (figure 8). Two methods of production were used, both involving the coating of a core (usually in copper or bronze, though for gold-plated coins sometimes in silver) with gold or silver alloy before striking took place. The core could be dipped in molten alloy to receive a thin wash of the precious metal, or alternatively a thin layer of gold or silver could be wrapped around the core and then hammered until it bonded with the base metal.

8. Plated forgery of a South Ferriby stater of the Corieltauvi. Traces of gold plating remain on the bronze core. (Institute of Archaeology, Oxford.)

The dies used to strike the forgeries may have been cast in a mould bearing the impression of a genuine coin, or a genuine coin may have been pressed into soft metal which was subsequently hardened to form the die; less convincing forgeries were produced simply by copying the design of a genuine die or coin on to a new die, in the latter case resulting in the reversal of the correct image. In some cases plated forgeries appear to have been officially sanctioned, since they were struck with dies also used for genuine coins.

The production of the cast bronze coinages of Kent and Dorset obviously required a different set of techniques. The Kentish types were technologically superior to the late Durotrigan coins and there is no reason to suggest a connection between the two. They were produced by pouring molten alloy into a set of moulds joined by runners, which could then be broken apart when the metal had cooled. The resulting coins often have parts of the sprue (the joining portion) projecting from the edge of the flan (figure 9).

The earliest examples of these coins have fine images which were presumably made by pressing an example of the prototype coinage (chapter 3) into the mould. On the 'Thurrock' variety (chapter 4) this process may have been repeated with successively less accurate copies, so that by the end of this series the images are effectively blobs of protruding metal (figure 18). On the succeeding flat linear potin type, the image was created by scribing a few simple lines in the clay of the mould (figure 9).

These coins are traditionally known as 'potins', the French term for a bronze alloy with a high (greater than 25 per cent) tin content. The Kentish coins generally have a tin content of 20-30 per cent with 3-5 per cent lead, and though 'potin' may be appropriate in some cases they are perhaps better described simply as cast bronzes. Control of their weight was difficult given the manufacturing method and, perhaps because people would have recognised this, clearly less important than for the struck coinages.

9. Cast bronze ('potin') coin from Kent. The remains of the sprue, the joining portion between moulds, can be seen projecting from the circular flan. (David Holman.)

The Durotrigan cast bronze coinage generally has a rather lower tin content (7-15 per cent) than the flat linear potin but was presumably produced in a very similar fashion. However, less effort was expended on the design, which is little more than a collection of dots (chapter 7).

3

The introduction of coinage to Britain

As we have seen, the first Celtic coins were imitations of the stater of Philip II of Macedon, brought back from the Mediterranean by mercenaries. These copies were not manufactured in Britain, although several have been found in the south-east of the country, including a particularly fine example from Kent (figure 1).

A number of other coins of this period have been found in Britain. They include a hoard of drachmae of the early second century BC produced in north Italy and reportedly discovered near Penzance, and several Carthaginian bronze coins of the fourth or third century, principally found in Kent (figure 10). These coins have traditionally been regarded as much later imports, arriving with the Romans or even dropped from the pockets of modern collectors, but – for the Carthaginian bronzes at least – enough have now been found in association with British Celtic coins to confirm that they arrived well before the Roman conquest.

Other very early imports include a few gold half and quarter staters produced in Belgica, now northern France, perhaps in the late third or early second century BC. These are closely modelled on coins of the Greek colonies of Tarentum (in southern Italy) and Syracuse (in Sicily), both of which also employed Celtic mercenaries. None of these early imports was imitated by the British Celts and, in the case of the bronze issues, they were presumably regarded as little more than interesting curiosities.

The first Celtic coinages to appear in quantity in Britain were also produced in Belgica. From the mid second century BC a succession of coins manufactured by the tribes of northern France was imported into the south-east of England. These are known in Britain as Gallo-Belgic A to F. The reasons why they were imported are still not fully understood. Traditionally, the coins were thought to have accompanied waves of Belgic invaders, but this explanation is no longer accepted; it is possible, though, that some were brought to the south-east by the Belgic raiders recorded by Caesar (*De Bello Gallico* V, 12), who perhaps settled in

10. Bronze coin of Carthage, found in Kent. (David Holman.)

11. Gallo-Belgic A, the large-flan gold stater. (Institute of Archaeology, Oxford.)

central southern Britain. However, it is not necessary to conjure up invasions unattested in the archaeological record to explain all of these coins. Their function undoubtedly varied, but at different times they are likely to have been used principally as payment for military service or mercenaries, and in exchanges between the elite of each society: in cementing political or social alliances, for example, or as gifts in a system of exchange bringing benefits to both sides. Caesar also comments (*De Bello Gallico* II, 4) that Diviciacus, king of the Suessiones in Belgic Gaul, previously had control over a large area of Britain and, if we can take him at his word, it would hardly be surprising to find that this intensive contact across the Channel involved the use of coinage.

The first of these imports – Gallo-Belgic A, also known as the large-flan stater – is one of the most beautiful of all Celtic coins (figure 11), displaying extraordinary detail in the flamboyant representation of the hair and the headdress. The basic influence of the stater of Philip II is still apparent, in the choice of a laurel-wreathed head and a horse as the main features of the design, but the portrayal of these elements is now unequivocally Celtic. This type was probably struck by the Ambiani, in the Somme valley.

Some political upheaval in their society may be reflected by the Gallo-Belgic B coinage, also known as the defaced-die type (figure 12). Both

12. Gallo-Belgic B, the defaced die stater. (Institute of Archaeology, Oxford.)

13. Gallo-Belgic C, the biface stater. (Institute of Archaeology, Oxford.)

staters and quarter staters were deliberately struck with defaced obverse dies, perhaps previously used for the Gallo-Belgic A series, and it has been suggested that its distribution in northern France – on the fringes of the territory of the Ambiani – might indicate the dissolution of that powerful kingdom. It is also possible that the staters were produced in Britain, since only quarter staters are recorded from the continent.

The first truly influential continental gold coinage followed these two series. Gallo-Belgic C (figure 13) was probably made from recalled Gallo-Belgic A coins between the early first century BC and about 60 BC, and it inspired a number of important British coinages which will be discussed in the next chapter. The series starts with an easily recognisable head on the obverse – still echoing the stater of Philip II – but the careful portrayal of the facial features is soon sacrificed in favour of emphasis on the laurel wreath, which becomes the focal point of most of the succeeding gold coinage. On the reverse the horse is a good deal simpler in style than on the preceding types, and the charioteer is reduced to little more than stylised arms and a collection of pellets; the legend too has now completely disappeared, to be replaced by a decorative pattern.

The Gallo-Belgic C stater is less common in Britain than the previous continental types but has a wider distribution, stretching from the Sussex coast to The Wash. Finds are particularly concentrated in Kent, and it is probable that some of the coins were produced there rather than on the continent. The same may be true for some elements of Gallo-Belgic E, the successor to C which was struck in colossal numbers between about 60 and 50 BC, in other words shortly before and then during the Gallic War. This is known as the uniface type (figure 14) since it lacks an obverse design; the horse is very similar to the Gallo-Belgic C type, and

14. Gallo-Belgic E, the uniface stater. (Institute of Archaeology, Oxford.)

indeed the earliest uniface coins can be die-linked to the last C-type staters, indicating that the same authority – traditionally thought to be the Ambiani – was responsible for the issue of both types. Although there is no way of establishing exactly how many coins were struck per die, it has been estimated that almost 1500 obverse dies were used for this series, which at a conservative figure of 1000 coins per die equates to 1,500,000 staters, containing almost 5000 kg of fine gold. The quantity of metal required for this output suggests that, in addition to recalling Gallo-Belgic C, the producers of the coins must have had use of other sources, for example torcs and other objects of treasure. The purity of the alloy was also deliberately reduced, so that more coins could be struck from less precious metal.

There can be little doubt that the production of this quantity of coins was fundamentally linked to the need to pay troops fighting Caesar. The presence of considerable numbers of the uniface coinage across Britain, from the south coast to the Humber, may thus confirm Caesar's comment (*De Bello Gallico* IV, 20) that Britain often supplied soldiers for campaigns in Gaul. It is also possible that some coins were imported by refugees from the war. The same process of introduction has been suggested for Gallo-Belgic D, since it has a predominantly coastal distribution in Britain. This type, struck only in quarter staters by an uncertain Belgic authority, has a curious design (figure 15) which has yet to be satisfactorily deciphered: it has been suggested that the obverse shows a boat with occupants, and the reverse a tree. In common with Gallo-Belgic C and (to a lesser extent) E, this coinage influenced several later British issues (chapter 4) and may in some cases have been an insular production itself.

15. Gallo-Belgic D quarter stater. The interpretation of the design remains a mystery: a boat with three occupants on one side, a tree on the other? (Institute of Archaeology, Oxford.)

The final Gallo-Belgic type to be considered here, class F or the triple-tailed horse stater (figure 16), was apparently struck by the Suessiones, to the east of Paris, at about the same time as Gallo-Belgic E. Although struck in far smaller quantities than the uniface stater, this type too had a very significant influence on the early British coinage, perhaps indicating a close relationship between the Suessiones and the population of central southern England. The obverse of the Gallo-Belgic F stater makes little attempt to retain a recognisable head but instead concentrates on the wreath and surrounding decoration. The reverse is

16. Gallo-Belgic F, the triple-tailed horse stater. (Institute of Archaeology, Oxford.)

characterised by the adoption of a triple-tailed horse, to be reproduced on much of the coinage of southern England in the next few decades.

Although the Gallo-Belgic issues C to F had an enormous and long-lasting influence on the early British coinage, archaeological evidence is increasingly demonstrating that the earliest British coinage of all was not one of the gold types based on Gallo-Belgic prototypes, perhaps produced around 70 BC, but a series of cast bronze or potin issues manufactured in Kent as many as thirty years or more previously. Once again the inspiration for this coinage must be sought in continental issues, but this time from further afield than Belgica. Bronze coins of the Greek colony of Massalia (Marseilles), dating to the late third or second century BC, were imitated in central Gaul (figure 17) and eventually – perhaps in the late second century BC – copied in Kent. These coins will be considered in more detail in the next chapter.

4

The first British coinages

The cast bronze coinage produced in Kent from the end of the second century BC took several forms. It seems that the earliest variety were the so-called Thurrock potins (figure 18), named after a hoard found at Thurrock in Essex. Metal-detector finds suggest, however, that its principal area of circulation was in Kent, though examples have been found as far west as the Isle of Wight and north to East Anglia and Lincolnshire. The earliest coins, usually weighing between 3 and 4 grams, are reasonably faithful copies of the continental issues (figure 17), bearing the head of Apollo on the obverse and a butting bull with

17. Cast bronze coin of southern Gaul, imitating issues of Massalia (Marseilles). (David Holman.)

MA (for Massalia) above on the reverse. Their design soon gives the impression of being hurriedly reproduced and eventually becomes barely recognisable (figure 18).

It is still not clear who issued these coins and for how long, nor do we know precisely what they were used for. But at some point, perhaps in the early years of the first century BC, they

18. Thurrock potins. The design was initially faithful to the continental prototype (above), but soon degenerated (below). (David Holman.)

19. Flat linear potin. The designs were probably based on the earlier Thurrock type. (Institute of Archaeology, Oxford.)

appear to have been replaced by a new style of flatter and lighter potin coinage. The first examples (figure 19) show some echoes of the earlier type, but again the designs are very rapidly stylised, with the head and the bull eventually represented by simple lines (figure 9). These coins can be broadly divided into two classes: a larger type, such as figures 9 and 19, and a smaller variety (figure 20), where the design reaches its ultimate degree of simplicity. It is not entirely clear if this division is valid beyond a simple physical difference in the coinage: the smaller type is probably later, but the physical change may also reflect a change in function or in issuing authority. Evidence is also increasing that the smaller potins are found predominantly to the north of the Thames, while the larger coins are mostly confined to Kent. Production of this coinage seems to have ended soon after the mid first

20. Late flat linear potin. The head and bull are now represented by a few simple lines. (David Holman.)

century BC and, although to some extent it overlapped with the first British gold coins, the types are not normally found together and are likely to have served very different functions in Celtic society.

While it is possible that some Gallo-Belgic C coins were produced in Kent, the first distinctively British derivatives from this coinage were struck not in Kent but both further to the west and also to the north of the Thames. The type known traditionally as British A or the Westerham stater (figure 21), probably produced from about 70 BC, is closely modelled on its Gallo-Belgic predecessor and may indeed have been

21. The Westerham stater (British A). The laurel leaves pointing downwards indicate that this coin belongs to the south Thames group. (Institute of Archaeology, Oxford.)

made from melted-down examples of the continental coinage. Two varieties are recognised, distinguished by the direction of the leaves in the laurel wreath: those with the leaves pointing upwards are generally found from the Thames northwards to East Anglia, and those with the leaves pointing downwards are found widely along the south coast and inland in Hampshire and Sussex. The south Thames type is rather lighter and consequently probably slightly later than its north Thames counterpart. Both types have traditionally been attributed to the Atrebates, but the distribution clearly demonstrates that they were produced by two different authorities.

Gallo-Belgic C also gave rise to other derivatives both north and south of the Thames. The Chute stater (British B) is found predominantly in Dorset, Wiltshire and Somerset. It has much the same design as British A, with the addition of small 'arms' to the pellet below the horse and a similar pellet above (figure 22). The reverse design is then copied on the Cheriton stater (British D; figure 5), centred on the hinterland of Portsmouth. This type and the Yarmouth stater (British C; figure 23), known principally from a hoard on the Isle of Wight, had no later derivatives and they may perhaps be regarded as the output of small *pagi* whose names are unknown to us.

To the north of the Thames, the Gallo-Belgic derived Clacton types (British F and G; figure 24) were probably struck from about 65 BC. Until

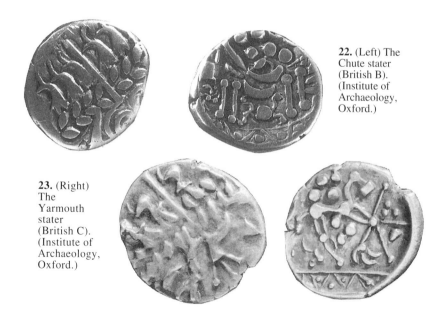

22. (Left) The Chute stater (British B). (Institute of Archaeology, Oxford.)

23. (Right) The Yarmouth stater (British C). (Institute of Archaeology, Oxford.)

24. (Left) The Clacton stater (British G). (Institute of Archaeology, Oxford.)

25. (Below) Quarter staters associated with the Clacton (British G) stater. (Institute of Archaeology, Oxford.)

the early 1990s these coins were known only from a hoard discovered at Clacton in 1898, but both have now become better represented as a result of discoveries made by metal-detector users. The British G type appears to have been accompanied by one or possibly two unusual quarter staters, both influenced by Gallo-Belgic D in the choice of obverse design (figure 25). Gallo-Belgic D also inspired several distinct varieties of coinage in the south, known collectively as British O (figure 26). Some of the British O quarter staters provided the models for part of the later Durotrigan tribal coinage (chapter 7).

Some elements of the Corieltauvian tribal coinage can also be traced back to Gallo-Belgic C. It provided the model for their first coinage, the north-east coast stater (British H and I; figure 27), and thus indirectly for the succeeding South Ferriby series (British K; chapter 8). As with the Clacton types, metal-detector discoveries are forcing reappraisal of the earliest coinage of this region, with the identification of a remarkably

26. The British O quarter stater. (Institute of Archaeology, Oxford.)

27. The north-
east coast stater
(British H).
(Institute of
Archaeology,
Oxford.)

cup-shaped (scyphate) coin – perhaps a quarter stater – occurring
predominantly in Lincolnshire (figure 28). Its origins, dating and
relationship to more mainstream coinages are as yet unknown.

In East Anglia development took a slightly different turn with the
replacement of the traditional horse by a dog or a wolf with particularly
fearsome jaws (British J; figure 29). The adoption of the wolf is typical of
the relatively slight modification to the Gallo-Belgic C prototype made by
the producers of all of these derivatives in the two decades or so before the
Gallic War. In contrast the developments which had the longest lasting
influence on British coin production took later Gallo-Belgic issues as their
model or broke away entirely to produce a uniquely British coinage.

To the north of the Thames, British L or the Whaddon Chase stater
(figure 30) was probably first struck during the Gallic War. It rapidly

28. (Left) Gold scyphate coin
found in Lincolnshire.
(Institute of Archaeology,
Oxford.)

29. (Left) The
Norfolk wolf
stater (British J).
(Institute of
Archaeology,
Oxford.)

30. The Whaddon
Chase stater (British L).
(Institute of
Archaeology, Oxford.)

dispensed with the head and the horse in the style of the earlier Gallo-Belgic issues and instead coupled a stylised representation of the laurel wreath with a much more realistic horse, struck to a new weight standard (initially 5.8 grams) and containing between 40 and 50 per cent gold. These coins are found widely in Buckinghamshire, Bedfordshire, Hertfordshire and Essex, with some more localised types possibly originating in East Anglia. Its influence extended on at least one occasion to the south of the Thames, where the Wonersh stater (British MA; figure 31) made a fleeting appearance in Sussex and Surrey.

By far the most influential coinage in the south, however, was the triple-tailed horse stater (British Q; figure 32), struck to much the same standard and with the same precious-metal content as the Whaddon Chase type, and also beginning during the Gallic War. This coinage

31. The Wonersh
stater (British MA).
(Institute of
Archaeology,
Oxford.)

32. The British
Q (Atrebatic)
stater.
(Institute of
Archaeology,
Oxford.)

33. The British QC (Atrebatic) quarter stater. (Institute of Archaeology, Oxford.)

was based not on Gallo-Belgic C but on Gallo-Belgic F of the Suessiones (figure 16), losing the triangular decoration below the wreath but otherwise initially faithful to the prototype. This type is found from the Sussex coast north through Surrey, east Hampshire, Berkshire and Oxfordshire and can reasonably be attributed to the Atrebates; it also provided the inspiration for British R, which formed the basis of the gold coinage of the Dobunni (chapter 7). In addition to the Atrebatic stater, which was eventually struck with a plain obverse, a long series of quarter staters was produced, displaying a bewildering variety of decoration around the central feature of the horse (figure 33).

The design of the Atrebatic stater was closely copied for the first inscribed coinage produced in Britain. The main themes of this south Thames development will be considered in the next chapter.

5

Coinage south of the Thames

The period immediately after Caesar's conquest of Gaul seems to have been a time of some confusion and readjustment amongst many of the peoples of the south Thames region. In the areas traditionally attributed to the Atrebates and Regni there were a great many localised silver issues, and even a short-lived bronze coinage (figure 34) closely modelled on a Belgic issue and apparently centred on Chichester. The proliferation of these generally rare coinages may perhaps be associated with the abrupt cessation of imports of gold from Gaul, now under Roman control. In Kent it seems that fairly small numbers of gold

34. Early coinage from the south Thames region: a silver 'Danebury' type (left) and a bronze coin (right) from Chichester. (Institute of Archaeology, Oxford.)

quarter staters were still produced in the first few years after the war (figure 35), while staters were extremely rare. It is likely that the last issues of potin coinage were also made around this time.

Within one or two decades of the end of the war, the situation in the territory of the Atrebates and Regni seems to have stabilised, with the appearance of the first British inscribed staters (figure 36). These coins closely resemble the uninscribed British Q staters (figure 32), with the addition of a COMMIOS inscription below and in front of the horse. Since at least the start of the seventeenth century, this Commius has

35. The trophy quarter stater (British P). The reverse design may be inspired by a coin of Julius Caesar. (David Holman.)

36. Gold stater of Commius. Part of the inscription is visible below and in front of the horse. (Institute of Archaeology, Oxford.)

been taken to be the same Gaulish chieftain who 'had rendered Caesar loyal and useful service in Britain' (*De Bello Gallico* VII, 76), where he was 'greatly respected' (*De Bello Gallico* IV, 21). Commius later turned against Caesar, however, and in 51 BC he was one of the leaders of the Gaulish force which attempted to relieve the siege at Alesia, the site of Caesar's victory over Vercingetorix. A year or so after the failure of that mission, following further skirmishes with Rome, Commius offered hostages to Antony 'as a guarantee that he would live where he was bidden and do as he was told' (*De Bello Gallico* VIII, 48). Antony is said to have accepted his petition, but rather than living 'where he was bidden' Commius is thought to have fled back to Britain in about 50 BC.

There are chronological problems in accepting this Commius as the Commius of the coins, if the claims of each of the later rulers in this region – Tincomarus, Eppillus and Verica – to be '*Commii filius*', or 'the son of Commius', are to be taken literally. If the phrase is intended simply as an indication of lineage, perhaps at one or two generations remove, then there is less of a problem, and it has now been convincingly demonstrated from early staters which read COM COMMIOS that the Commius who issued the coins is likely to have been the son of Caesar's Commius. He may also have struck issues in silver, linked to a very rare variety of the stater by a sort of E symbol above the horse (figure 37).

The first coins of Commius' successor, Tincomarus, retain the characteristically Celtic design of the earlier staters (figure 38). But late in the first century BC a radical change was made to the coinage which must reflect much closer ties between the southern British kingdom and

37. Silver unit perhaps of Commius. The meaning of the 'E' symbol above the horse, which sometimes appears on its side, is unknown. (Institute of Archaeology, Oxford.)

38. Staters of Tincomarus. The earlier type (above) maintains the Celtic style of his predecessor but is then replaced by a much more Romanised design (below). The correct name of this ruler, previously thought to be Tincommius, was learnt only in 1996, when a few coins on which it was visible in full were found amongst two iron age coin hoards discovered at Alton in Hampshire. (Institute of Archaeology, Oxford.)

Rome. A new classically inspired design was issued (figure 38), so thoroughly Romanised in its appearance that it has been suggested that the coins were struck from Roman-engraved dies. Further evidence of this close association is provided by metal analyses of the accompanying silver units (figure 39), which not only adopt classical motifs for their design but are struck in virtually the same alloy as contemporary Roman denarii; in other words, imported Roman denarii almost certainly provided the bullion for these coins.

The coins of Tincomarus are concentrated in the southern part of the territory of the Atrebates and Regni, perhaps originating from Chichester. Tincomarus seems not to have held control over the northern territory centred on Calleva (Silchester), where Eppillus – who also claimed to be a son of Commius – struck coins announcing himself to be the king of Calleva (figure 40). The means by which Eppillus came to hold this

39. (Left) Silver unit of Tincomarus, possibly struck from imported Roman denarii. (Institute of Archaeology, Oxford.)

40. (Right) Silver unit of Eppillus, described as REX CALL, the king of Calleva. (Institute of Archaeology, Oxford.)

41. Bronze unit of Eppillus, struck for use in Kent. (Institute of Archaeology, Oxford.)

position are uncertain, as are the precise dates of his rule, though a reign of ten or fifteen years around the turn of the millennium may be appropriate. Either simultaneously with or after his control of Calleva, Eppillus also held land in north-east Kent, for which he authorised a separate series of coins, including several bronze issues (figure 41), a metal and denomination unknown in the Silchester area. Perhaps the control of two areas overstretched Eppillus' resources, for around AD 10 he was replaced at Calleva by Verica – the third putative son of Commius – who brought together both southern and northern parts of the territory for the first time. Tincomarus is believed to have fled to Rome to seek the protection of Augustus at much the same period.

Verica continued and developed the tradition of using classical models for most of his coinage. His early staters recall those of Tincomarus in the use of a tablet with inscription and a horseman bearing a spear; later coins feature a superbly engraved vine-leaf on the obverse (figure 42). The silver types – units and minims – display an enormous variety of motifs borrowed from classical coins and, possibly, gemstones: sphinxes, Roman busts and cornucopiae (horns of plenty), for example (figure 43).

Verica's long period of control in the south Thames region seems to have waned in the AD 30s, under the pressure of invaders from the north of the Thames. Epaticcus,

42. (Above) Gold stater of Verica. (Institute of Archaeology, Oxford.)

43. (Right) Silver unit of Verica, with cornucopiae on the obverse. (Institute of Archaeology, Oxford.)

recorded on his coins as the son of Tasciovanus (and hence the brother of Cunobelin; chapter 6), gained control of the Calleva region and produced a short series of staters, silver units and minims (figure 44). He was followed very briefly by Caratacus, son of Cunobelin, who is believed to have issued silver units (almost identical in design to those of Epaticcus)

44. Silver unit of Epaticcus (left) and silver minim probably of Caratacus (right). (Institute of Archaeology, Oxford.)

and minims inscribed CARA (figure 44), in the short period before retreating to Wales in the face of Claudius' invasion of AD 43.

Verica is thought to be the Berikos recorded by Dio Cassius (*Roman History* LX, 19) who fled to Rome in about AD 42 to seek assistance from Claudius and thus provided the emperor with a pretext for invading Britain. Following the Roman invasion, Cogidubnus was installed as the client king of the Regni and Roman coinage soon became widespread in the south Thames region.

As we have already seen, Eppillus struck coins for use in northern Kent for a short period at the start of the first century AD. The development of non-potin coinage in Kent before this period is not well understood, largely because the coins themselves are generally very rare. Caesar famously records four kings in Kent – Cingetorix, Carvilius,

45. Silver units of Dubnovellaunus. The unique coin on the left has three horses' heads and forelegs forming the starfish-like design on the obverse, with Dubnovellaunus' name around the edge of the flan. The coin on the right betrays Roman influence in its portrayal of a seated metalworker. (Ashmolean Museum, Oxford; Institute of Archaeology, Oxford.)

Taximagulus and Segovax – but we have no idea if any of them were responsible for the uninscribed coins (figure 35) issued at the time of the Gallic War or shortly afterwards. The most significant producer of

46. (Left) Gold quarter stater of Vosenios (above) and a bronze coin perhaps issued by the same ruler (below), bearing the inscription SA. (Institute of Archaeology, Oxford; David Holman.)

47. (Below) Plated silver unit of Amminus. The DVN below the Pegasus may refer to the site of the mint. (David Holman.)

coins in the four decades before the involvement of Eppillus was a Dubnovellaunus, apparently not the same Dubnovellaunus who controlled some of the north Thames region at approximately the same time (chapter 6). The style of some of these coins – notably a marvellous and unique silver unit found in north-east Kent (figure 45) – is quintessentially Celtic, suggesting a date perhaps around 40 or 30 BC. Other issues of Dubnovellaunus adopt Roman designs (figure 45) and were probably produced later in the century, once again reflecting increasing contact between the south-east of the country and Roman Gaul.

Coins apparently issued by a Vosenios probably belong sometime at the end of this period. So also, though they too might be of Vosenios, do those of a ruler recorded only as SA (figure 46). These letters need not refer to a personal name but could instead record a title, the site of a mint or the name of an unrecorded group of people. Only further discoveries and archaeological investigation are likely to provide more information on these matters.

Following the disappearance of Eppillus in the early years of the first century AD, the coinage of Cunobelin circulated in Kent, with some issues apparently minted specifically for use south of the Thames (chapter 6). Coinage of Kentish origin was very briefly revived late in Cunobelin's reign by Amminus, son of Cunobelin, who seems to have been installed in Kent by his father. He produced small issues of silver and bronze units largely based on earlier designs of Cunobelin (figure 47), before his expulsion from Britain in AD 39 or 40 and the Roman conquest in AD 43 halted insular coin production in the south-east.

6
Coinage north of the Thames

In some respects the first stages in the development of north Thames coinage after the Gallic War echo those in southern Britain. Again there is a problem of identity at the start of the series. Cassivellaunus, Caesar tells us (*De Bello Gallico* V, 11), was the king of a north Thames tribe who had previously killed the king of the Trinovantes and driven his son Mandubracius to seek refuge with Caesar but was elected the leader of the British resistance to Rome in 54 BC. After his stronghold north of the Thames had been overrun, Cassivellaunus successfully sued Caesar for peace, using Commius as an intermediary (*De Bello Gallico* V, 22). It is possible, but as yet unproven, that Cassivellaunus was at the head of the tribe – perhaps the Catuvellauni? – who produced the Whaddon Chase staters (figure 30) found in numbers to the north of the Thames. Like the Atrebatic uninscribed staters, these were eventually struck with obliterated obverse dies and, again as in the south, a number of rare silver types (figure 48) seem to have been produced at much the same time. A further point of comparison is provided by two early struck bronze coinages from Essex and Suffolk, recalling if not in type then at least in nature the issue from the Chichester area (figure 34). The north Thames types (figure 48) had been identified as British in the late nineteenth century but more recently were thought to be continental imports; metal-detector discoveries have now confirmed their British origins.

The first inscribed coinage to emerge in this period in the north Thames region is that of Addedomaros, produced perhaps from around 35 BC. He issued gold staters and quarter staters, and silver and bronze units. Only the gold and a few of the silver coins are inscribed and thus the

48. Early coinage from the north Thames region: silver (above) and bronze (below) units of uncertain attribution. (Institute of Archaeology, Oxford.)

49. (Left) Bronze coin perhaps of Addedomaros. (Institute of Archaeology, Oxford.)

50. (Below) Gold stater of Addedomaros. The first letters of his name are visible behind the tail of the horse. (Institute of Archaeology, Oxford.)

attribution of some of the silver and bronze remains in doubt (figure 49). The design of the staters is clearly based on the earlier Whaddon Chase coinage, retaining a similar horse but with ADDEDOMAROS – spelt in various forms, with

the first two Ds as thetas – around the edge of the flan (figure 50).

The distribution of Addedomaros' coins suggests that he may have been the leader of the Trinovantes, though it is possible that he ruled a greater area than the later tribal territory. Roughly contemporary with him is Tasciovanus, who began to strike coinage with a slightly more westerly distribution, focused on Verulamium (St Albans), which appears to have been his principal mint (figure 51). His coins initially maintain the Celtic theme of the Whaddon Chase series, again concentrating on the stylised wreath and seemingly incorporating a hidden face in the design (figure 52). A change is signalled later in the first century BC by the adoption of Romanised types, particularly on the silver and bronze

51. (Left) Silver unit of Tasciovanus. VER on the obverse indicates the mint of Verulamium. (Institute of Archaeology, Oxford.)

52. (Right) Gold stater of Tasciovanus. The decoration on the obverse appears to incorporate hidden faces. (Institute of Archaeology, Oxford.)

53. (Above) Gold quarter stater of Tasciovanus, struck at Camulodunum. Part of the CAMVL monogram can be seen above the head of the horse. (Institute of Archaeology, Oxford.)

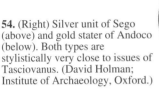

54. (Right) Silver unit of Sego (above) and gold stater of Andoco (below). Both types are stylistically very close to issues of Tasciovanus. (David Holman; Institute of Archaeology, Oxford.)

coinages, although their stylistic range is restricted in comparison to his south Thames contemporary, Tincommius (chapter 5).

A very rare early gold type and accompanying quarter stater issued by Tasciovanus appear to have been minted not at Verulamium but at Camulodunum (Colchester; figure 53). This may indicate that for a brief period Tasciovanus held the territory to the east of his own kingdom; the CAMVL inscription does not recur later in his coinage. Towards the end of his reign, however, several small-scale issues appear bearing names associated with that of Tasciovanus: Andoco, Sego, Dias and Rues. Issues in gold, silver and bronze are known for Andoco and Sego (figure 54), in silver and bronze for Dias, and solely in bronze for Rues. Although an attempt has been made to place these rulers – presuming that they are all personal names – in a single chronological sequence, it is probably more likely that they were associates of or subordinates to Tasciovanus, perhaps occupying small areas or *pagi* within the territory under his overall control. Perhaps another hint at this situation is provided by the RICON inscription added to his later gold coinage (figure 55),

55. Gold stater of Tasciovanus, described as RICON or king. (Institute of Archaeology, Oxford.)

equivalent to the Latin REX, emphasising his position as king of the tribe. In the east of the north Thames region Addedomaros appears to have been succeeded by Dubnovellaunus, whose coins are very clearly concentrated in Essex. He does not seem to be the same Dubnovellaunus who issued coins in Kent (chapter 5). A link is provided to his predecessor's coinage by the use of a palm branch, associated with the Roman goddess of victory, on the reverse of his staters (figure 56). He also struck silver and bronze in relatively small numbers. The palm branch then reappears on the last coinage in the north Thames region, that of Cunobelin, described by Suetonius (*Lives of the Caesars* XLIV, 2) as '*Britannorum rex*', 'the king of the Britons'.

56. Gold stater of
Dubnovellaunus.
(Institute of
Archaeology,
Oxford.)

Cunobelin, recorded on some of his coins as the son of Tasciovanus, united the territories of the Trinovantes and the Catuvellauni to form the most powerful kingdom in Celtic Britain for the three decades before the Roman conquest, extending his influence south of the Thames and, so Dio Cassius tells us (*Roman History* LX, 20), westwards to the territory of the Dobunni. Whether he achieved this by force, by diplomacy or perhaps by the adroit combination of both is unknown. His first gold staters and quarter staters (figure 57) bear the name of the Camulodunum mint prominently displayed on the obverse, backed with a superb representation of the two-horse chariot or *biga* (which Caesar had encountered in Britain, much to his surprise, sixty years before). These are rare coins, perhaps to be associated with Cunobelin's accession to the throne. The succeeding gold coinage adopts an ear of corn or barley as the defining feature of the obverse, with CAMV indicating the mint,

57. The *biga* stater
of Cunobelin.
(Institute of
Archaeology,
Oxford.)

coupled with a single horse and the first three or four letters of Cunobelin's name; this coinage remains relatively static throughout the reign, the most significant change being the adoption of a more Romanised horse on the later issues (figure 58).

58. The 'classic' stater of Cunobelin. (Institute of Archaeology, Oxford.)

Cunobelin's silver and bronze coinage is initially Celtic in design (figure 59) and, like the first gold coinage, is mostly very rare. This may reflect a relative lack of bullion available at the start of Cunobelin's reign, or perhaps simply little requirement for these denominations. As Cunobelin consolidated his hold over the north Thames territory and intensified contact with Roman Gaul, so the amount of coinage produced increased considerably and, in a familiar pattern, turned to classical prototypes for many of its designs. Although Roman Republican or Augustan coins provide the models for many, other older and more

59. Early silver unit of Cunobelin. (David Holman.)

obscure Mediterranean coins were also used: for example, the standing soldier on a bronze type (figure 60), copied from a coin issued at Aitna in Sicily some time after 210 BC. In some cases, such as this rare and localised issue from Aitna, it is difficult to imagine how Cunobelin's die-engravers came into contact with the prototype, and yet there can be very

60. Bronze unit of Cunobelin, with a standing soldier on the obverse copied from a coin from Sicily. (Institute of Archaeology, Oxford.)

61. Bronze core of a forged quarter stater of Cunobelin (above), found in Kent, and a bronze unit of Cunobelin (below) of a type probably issued for use in Kent. (David Holman.)

little doubt that they were able to study this coin and produce a realistic copy more than two hundred years after it had circulated in a small area of the classical world.

Cunobelin's influence undoubtedly extended south of the Thames, for his coins are found widely in Kent. His quarter staters were forged there (figure 61) and it is even possible that some bronze issues were specifically produced for use south of the river: this is most likely to have been so for the bronze coin which bears a Pegasus with the CAM mint name on the obverse and a Roman figure of Victory on the reverse (figure 61), three-quarters of which have been found in Kent. As we have already seen (chapter 5), Cunobelin apparently installed one of his sons, Amminus, in Kent, where he produced a small issue of silver and bronze coinage based closely on his father's, perhaps in the middle 30s AD.

Cunobelin may have also played a part in the seizure by his brother Epaticcus of the northern part of the Atrebatic territory, around Calleva, in the same decade; Epaticcus may perhaps be indicating his loyalty to the greater north Thames cause through his use of the corn-ear on his gold coinage (figure 62). His successor for the brief period before the Roman invasion was Cunobelin's son Caratacus, who fled to Wales with another son, Togodumnus, following the Claudian invasion.

We have no idea yet whether either of these brothers can be linked to a very rare issue of quarter staters and silver units bearing an A or AGR, which may be associated with the brief period between Cunobelin's death, thought to have occurred in AD 41 or 42, and the invasion of AD 43. As with so many aspects of this coinage, the tantalising glimpses offered of the situation in south-east Britain at the end of the iron age cannot yet be merged into a full picture.

62. Gold stater of Epaticcus, recorded as TASCI F, 'the son of Tasciovanus'. (Institute of Archaeology, Oxford.)

63. Uninscribed gold stater of the Dobunni (British R). (Institute of Archaeology, Oxford.)

7
The western periphery

The two most powerful late iron age kingdoms, north and south of the Thames, were surrounded by a broad arc of so-called peripheral tribes who were either prevented from direct interaction with Roman Gaul by their marginal position or who deliberately retained an anti-Roman stance throughout the last century of their independence. In both cases this had a considerable impact on the development of their coinage, which can be very broadly summed up as a lack of the Romanising influence so common on the coinages of the Atrebates, the Trinovantes and the Catuvellauni in the late first century BC and early first century AD. In this chapter we will examine the coinages of the Durotriges and the Dobunni, who occupied the section of this arc from the Dorset coast north through Somerset and west Wiltshire to Gloucestershire, Herefordshire and Worcestershire.

The earliest coinage attributed to the Dobunni is almost identical to the uninscribed British Q stater (figure 32), with the addition of the tree-like symbol on the obverse common to almost all of the succeeding gold coinage (figure 63). The interpretation of this motif is uncertain, but its persistence presumably indicates its importance to the Dobunni. An uninscribed quarter stater (figure 64) is traditionally associated with this stater, but provenances are few and far between and it may perhaps be an Atrebatic production.

Following the uninscribed coinage is a series of inscribed staters,

64. Uninscribed gold quarter stater, perhaps of the Dobunni. (Institute of Archaeology, Oxford.)

65. Gold stater of
Bodvoc. (Institute of
Archaeology, Oxford.)

some with associated silver units, as well as a number of uninscribed silver units which are more difficult to match with the rulers identified on the gold coinage. The metrology and metallurgy of the gold staters suggest that either Bodvoc or Corio was the first ruler to add his name to the coinage, in Bodvoc's case unusually replacing the tree symbol (figure 65). These coins contain about 48 per cent gold, significantly more than any of the other inscribed Dobunnic issues, which average between 40 and 42 per cent. Corio also issued a very rare quarter stater, virtually identical in its reverse type to the problematic uninscribed issue mentioned above (figure 64), but with COR inscribed on the plain

obverse. It is possible that Bodvoc and Corio ruled different parts of the Dobunnic territory simultaneously, since Corio's coins are found throughout the region, while Bodvoc's are clearly concentrated in the north.

Corio did not add his name to the silver coinage – one or more of the uninscribed types may belong to him – while Bodvoc issued a very different silver type (figure 66), possibly drawing its obverse inspiration from a coin of Tasciovanus, and thus perhaps indicative of a political realignment from the southern to

66. Silver units of the Dobunni: Bodvoc (top), uninscribed early (middle) and late (bottom). (Institute of Archaeology, Oxford.)

67. Silver units perhaps produced between the territory of the Dobunni and the Atrebates. The coin on the right bears winged motifs on its reverse similar to those on the Whaddon Chase stater. (Institute of Archaeology, Oxford.)

the northern kingdom sometime in the late first century BC. It stands out clearly from the rest of the silver coinage, which begins with a stylised though well-drawn head on the obverse and ultimately becomes a barely recognisable jumble of pellets and lines (figure 66). The earliest coins in this series have a distribution rather at odds with much of the later coinage. They are found in some numbers in eastern Wiltshire, west Berkshire and south-west Oxfordshire, where the mainstream Dobunnic silver is very rare. Also concentrated in this area are a number of so-called 'irregular types' (figure 67) and a growing number of previously unknown varieties recovered by metal-detector users which appear to be derived both from the earliest Dobunnic silver and from some of the early Atrebatic uninscribed silver (chapter 5). One new type is particularly intriguing (figure 67), as it includes in its design several examples of the winged motif found above the horse on the Whaddon Chase staters (figure 30); it may perhaps be another indication of contact with the north Thames kingdom.

It thus seems likely that a group distinct from either the Atrebates or the Dobunni produced its own coinage in this area in the late first century BC, drawing on influences from the several 'tribal' coinages it encountered. They may also have been responsible for the Savernake stater (British MB; figure 68), a curious uninscribed issue in very base gold, which bears a horse similar in style to many of the silver units found in this area.

Returning to the more regular Dobunnic coinage, it appears that Bodvoc and Corio were succeeded by Comux and Catti, who may perhaps be

68. The Savernake base gold stater (British MB). (Institute of Archaeology, Oxford.)

69. Gold stater of Eisv.
(Institute of Archaeology,
Oxford.)

responsible for some of the later uninscribed silver (such as figure 66).
Comux's staters are very rare and thus little can be said about their
distribution. Catti's staters are rather more common, with a
predominantly northern distribution recalling that of Bodvoc. Again it
is possible that these leaders ruled different parts of the Dobunnic territory
at the same time.

The last two Dobunnic rulers named on the gold coinage are Eisv
(figure 69) and Anted, who also added their names to the silver issues
(figure 70). Their coinages are both spread widely across the whole of
the Dobunnic territory, leaving little doubt that one followed the other –
probably Anted then Eisv – in authority.

The illustrations of the mainstream Dobunnic coinage show clearly
how static it was in comparison to the Romanised coinages of the
south-eastern core. To the south-west of the Dobunni, the Durotriges
produced an even more immobilised coinage. The principal denomination

70. (Right) Silver unit of Anted. (Institute
of Archaeology, Oxford.)

71. (Left) Silver
stater of the
Durotriges.
(Institute of
Archaeology,
Oxford.)

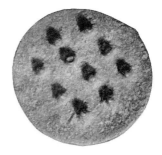

72. Cast bronze coin of the Durotriges. (Institute of Archaeology, Oxford.)

was the stater, based closely on British A (figure 21) despite the fact that British B was much more common on Durotrigan territory. This type was debased fairly rapidly from good silver (about 80 per cent) containing a small amount of gold (figure 71) to base silver and eventually bronze; silver-plated coins with a bronze core were also common. The disappearance of silver from the Durotrigan stater coinage probably reflects changes to the dominant trade route through Gaul in the wake of Caesar's conquest: the Atlantic coastal route which favoured the south-west peninsula lost ground to the northern Gaul/south-eastern Britain axis, which was so successfully exploited by the south and north Thames kingdoms. Nevertheless trade to and from the south-west continued, and it may be in connection with this that a series of cast bronze coins was produced, probably in the early first century AD (figure 72). These coins were based on the struck bronze staters, bearing a simple pattern of dots on each side and thus representing the ultimate debasement of the stater of Philip II of Macedon which had provided the inspiration for the first Celtic coins more than three centuries earlier. They were probably produced at Hengistbury Head on the south coast of Dorset, since almost every example has been found within 5 miles (8 km) of Hengistbury, and the site has provided excavated evidence of bronze metalworking in the late iron age and early Roman period.

Although the struck bronze coinage was by far the commonest issue of the Durotriges, they also produced a rather more inventive range of silver quarter staters. These were initially identical in design to the British O gold quarter staters (figure 26), which had themselves developed from Gallo-Belgic D (figure 15). As with the staters, the first few coins contained some gold and were equally rapidly debased, but, unlike the stater series, production seems to have ceased when the supply of silver dried up; examples in bronze, aside from silver-plated cores, are rare. The obverse design on the quarter stater

                                         Celtic Coinage in Britain

73. Silver quarter staters of the Durotriges. (Institute of Archaeology, Oxford.)

gradually faded to create an almost uniface coinage, while the reverse went through several modifications, though retaining the central zigzag line (figure 73). A separate variety of quarter stater may have developed from the uniface type, with the re-establishment of an obverse design sometimes described as a starfish (figure 73). Alternatively, as the starfish-type coins are generally struck in better silver, they may be another early offshoot from the British O type.

The quarter-stater coinage probably ceased a couple of decades before the turn of the millennium, presumably at much the same time as the staters became wholly bronze. Both the struck and the cast bronze coinages have been found in great numbers in post-conquest hoards, alongside Roman coins, indicating that they may have circulated for some considerable time after the invasion of AD 43.

8
The northern periphery

The territory to the north of the kingdoms of the Trinovantes and the Catuvellauni was dominated by two tribes: the Corieltauvi (formerly known as the Coritani), centred on Lincolnshire and also occupying parts of Northamptonshire, Leicestershire, Nottinghamshire and Yorkshire; and the Iceni, concentrated in Norfolk and neighbouring parts of Cambridgeshire and Suffolk. Like the western peripheral tribes discussed in the previous chapter, neither tribe shows much evidence of Romanisation in its coinage, but, unlike the Dobunni and the Durotriges, the types and designs are considerably less static.

The Corieltauvian coinage throughout the later first century BC seems to have been uninscribed. The north-east coast staters (figure 27), based like so many other early British coinages on Gallo-Belgic C, were succeeded by the South Ferriby type (figure 8), named after a hoard found on the south bank of the Humber in the early twentieth century. On the obverse of these coins the wreath is enlarged to fill most of the flan. On the reverse the horse is engraved in a striking fashion, the body represented by a series of broad crescents barely touching one another, the head by a large triangle; the legs are usually curved above the knee, represented by a pellet, and straight below. The charioteer has become wholly stylised; below the horse is usually a star. Variants of this type, struck in baser gold, replace the star with a spiral and bear a rectangular or rhomboid box above the horse, usually containing four pellets (figure 74).

No quarter staters are known for this coinage, but the staters are accompanied by silver units and half-units, also found in numbers at South Ferriby. These begin with a finely engraved boar – possibly copied from a Roman denarius – backed with an equally fine horse

74. Gold 'kite type' stater of the Corieltauvi. (Institute of Archaeology, Oxford.)

75. Silver units of the
Corieltauvi. (Institute of
Archaeology, Oxford.)

(figure 75). Around the boar and the horse a bewildering range of
decorative variation is introduced, but eventually both central features
and surrounding motifs become much simplified (figure 75); the obverse
dies are used until worn smooth.

This coinage probably circulated until around the turn of the
millennium. Early in the first century AD the Corieltauvi began to add
inscriptions, probably the names of their leaders, to the coinage,
beginning with VEP, whose staters are otherwise almost identical to the
preceding South Ferriby type. These coins were followed by issues
inscribed AVN AST or AVN COST (figure 76), struck in the familiar
combination of staters, silver units and silver half-units. Evidence for
the minting of these three denominations on Corieltauvian territory has
been provided by the enormous quantities of mould trays excavated at
Old Sleaford in Lincolnshire, in three sizes (chapter 2).

The order of the inscribed coins following this point is not yet
definitively established and is complicated by the possibility of rulers in
different areas of this large territory issuing coins at the same time; as in

76. Silver unit of AVN COST.
Part of the inscription is visible
above the horse. (Institute of
Archaeology, Oxford.)

77. Silver unit of VEP CORF (above) and gold stater of ESVP RASV (below). (Institute of Archaeology, Oxford.)

other cases we ought not to assume an uninterrupted sequence of rulers based in one location. Inscribed coins in the names of ESVP RASV (figure 77) and VEP CORF (perhaps meaning VEP the son of COR; figure 77), the latter a particularly large series, maintain very similar designs in the same denominations, with the addition of silver minims for VEP CORF.

The other inscribed coinages are generally rarer and display more significant modification to the design. Inscriptions are added to the obverse of staters and silver units (figure 78), and the horse, while recognisably Corieltauvian, has a differently formed head. Complete ranges of stater, unit and half-unit are less common and the rarest issues may well relate to the period of the Roman invasion.

To the south-east of the Corieltauvi lay the Iceni, producers of by far the most vigorous and inventive of the Celtic coinages of the peripheral tribes. Their talent for innovation in Celtic design had already been demonstrated by the adoption of the wolf on their version of the Gallo-Belgic C stater (figure 29), and it was maintained throughout much of their early coinage. The Norfolk wolf staters were replaced, perhaps around 40 BC, by the group collectively known as the Freckenham type (British N). This is a complicated coinage, displaying several varieties of obverse design coupled with a relatively static horse surrounded by

78. Silver unit of VOLISOS CARTIVEL (above) and gold stater of DVMNOC TIGIR SENO (below). (Institute of Archaeology, Oxford.)

many different arrangements of pellets, wheels and other motifs (figure 79). Quarter staters were also produced, known as the Irstead type; another quarter stater of the same general period (figure 80), known only through metal-detector discoveries, bears a wreath on the obverse which hints at a relationship with the producers of the north Thames British A coinage.

79. (Right) Gold stater of the Freckenham type (British N). (Institute of Archaeology, Oxford.)

80. (Below) Early gold quarter staters associated with the Iceni: the Irstead type (left) and a newly discovered type (right). (Institute of Archaeology, Oxford.)

81. Unique silver unit perhaps of
the Iceni. (Institute of
Archaeology, Oxford.)

During this period a number of silver types were introduced to the region. Some are seemingly one-offs (figure 81), perhaps produced by authorities with very limited resources or for some very specific purpose. The main series of this time, known as the Bury types, bears a head with an intricate diadem and a fine horse; both sides carry numerous decorative motifs which may perhaps have had special significance for their users (figure 82). Also early are the first of the group known as the face/horse series (figure 82), bearing heads quite unlike those on any other British Celtic coinage.

82. Early silver units of the Iceni: the Bury type (above) and the early face/horse type (below). (Institute of Archaeology, Oxford.)

This early face/horse type seems to have been followed by the normal face/horse coinage (figure 83), in its later style apparently showing a man with a moustache. It has been suggested that this was the coinage of Boudicca, but it seems likely to be much earlier, not least because it would be very unusual to find a major series of uninscribed coinage – such as this – issued after an even longer series of inscribed coins which must predate the Boudiccan rebellion (described below). Approximately

Celtic Coinage in Britain

83. The normal face/horse silver unit
of the Iceni. (Institute of
Archaeology, Oxford.)

concurrent with the normal face/horse coins is a series pairing a boar
and a horse. The first of these (figure 84) are so similar in style to some
Freckenham staters that the same die-cutter must have been responsible
for both the gold and the silver types. One of the regular boar/horse
types bears the inscription CAN DVRO, of uncertain meaning; this
may be the earliest inscribed Icenian type.

The switch to inscribed issues corresponds to a major change in the
design of the coinage, with the adoption of an obverse pattern based on
back-to-back crescents. This is carried throughout the succeeding pattern/

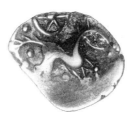

84. Early boar/horse silver unit of
the Iceni. (Institute of
Archaeology, Oxford.)

horse coinage, both on gold and silver, and the obverses of the three
inscribed stater types listed below, all of which are very rare, are produced
from the same dies, indicating that they are all roughly contemporary
and perhaps the issues of rulers of different parts of the Icenian territory.
The first types bear the legend ANTED in the form of a monogram
below the horse, on both the stater (figure 85) and silver units (figure
86) and half-units. Virtually identical types were produced with the

85. Gold stater of
ANTED of the Iceni.
(Institute of
Archaeology, Oxford.)

86. (Left) Silver units of the Iceni: ANTED (above) and ECEN (below). (Institute of Archaeology, Oxford.)

87. (Right) Silver units of the Iceni: ECE (above) and SAENV (below). (Institute of Archaeology, Oxford.)

inscription ECEN (figure 86). While it might seem likely that this should be a version of the tribal name, other instances in the Celtic world of the name of the tribe appearing on their coinage are extremely rare, and thus ECEN may refer to an individual.

The ECEN inscription is blundered on the following coinage to ED or EDN and is eventually dropped altogether, replaced by a variety of symbols. The succeeding type carries the legend ECE and shows a significant modification to the horse's head (figure 87), probably copied from a bronze coin of Cunobelin which bears a horse with its head turned towards the viewer. The horse's head is later modified to an upturned Y shape.

The last two truly Celtic issues of the Iceni are identical to the later ECE type, but with the legends AESV and SAENV (figure 87) below the horse. These are much less common than the remainder of the pattern/horse coinages, of which many thousands are known from a series of hoards found in East Anglia, mostly discovered with the aid of metal detectors and some regrettably undeclared. These hoards are traditionally associated with the Boudiccan rebellion in AD 60-1, though some may have been buried at other times in the seventeen-year period between the Claudian invasion and Boudicca's revolt; a minor rebellion is recorded by Tacitus (*Annals* XIV, 32) in AD 47-8, for example. During this time the Iceni formed a client kingdom under the leadership

88. Silver unit of the client king
Prasutagus, of the Iceni. (Institute of
Archaeology, Oxford.)

of Prasutagus, who issued possibly the last British Celtic coinage (figure 88). Here at last is evidence of significant Romanisation on the Icenian coinage: the traditional style replaced by a Roman bust and a more realistic horse; the inscription, SVB RI PRASTO ESICO FECIT ('under King Prasto, Esico made me'), uniquely recording the names of both the moneyer and the king. These coins are extremely rare in comparison to the previous Icenian types and thus seem unlikely to have circulated widely in the client kingdom.

Following Prasutagus' death in AD 59 or 60 Rome attempted to complete the process of absorbing the Icenian kingdom into the British province. Prasutagus' will, in which he had made his two daughters joint heirs with the emperor, was disregarded: his daughters were raped and his wife, Boudicca, flogged, and the Iceni rose in rebellion against the Roman army. The Trinovantes and other unnamed tribes joined forces with Boudicca and destroyed London, Colchester and St Albans before facing the Roman commander, Suetonius Paulinus, in battle. Tacitus (*Annals* XIV, 37) records that 'It was a glorious victory equal to those of the good old days: some estimate as many as eighty thousand British dead... Boudicca ended her life with poison.'

There was little place in the newly subdued province for Celtic coinage. Excavations of early Roman settlements indicate that silver and bronze coins circulated for another generation or two, but production was finished. The last great flourish of Celtic coinage had ended, finally succumbing to the power of Rome.

9
Further reading

Allen, D.F. 'A Study of the Dobunnic Coinage' in E.M. Clifford, *Bagendon: A Belgic Oppidum.* Heffer, 1961.

Allen, D.F. *The Coins of the Coritani.* Oxford University Press, 1963.

Allen, D.F. 'The Chronology of Durotrigan Coinage' in I.A. Richmond, *Hod Hill* volume II. British Museum Press, 1967.

Allen, D.F. 'The Coins of the Iceni', *Britannia* 1 (1970), 1-33.

Allen, D.F., and Nash, D. *The Coins of the Ancient Celts.* Edinburgh University Press, 1980. A general introduction to Celtic coinage, both British and continental, with extensive lists of further reading.

Bean, S. *The Coinage of the Atrebates and Regni.* Oxford University Committee for Archaeology, 2000.

Creighton, J. *Coins and Power in Late Iron Age Britain.* Cambridge University Press, 2000. A thought-provoking study of the Iron Age/ Roman transition in Britain and the evidence provided by coinage.

Cunliffe, B.W. *Iron Age Britain.* Batsford, 1995. An introduction to the society in which British Celtic coins were used.

Haselgrove, C.C. 'The Archaeology of British Potin Coinage', *Archaeological Journal* 145 (1988), 99–122.

Haselgrove, C.C. 'The Development of British Iron-Age Coinage', *Numismatic Chronicle* 153 (1993), 31–64.

Hobbs, R. *British Iron Age Coins in the British Museum.* British Museum Press, 1996. Fully illustrated catalogue of more than 4500 coins, with a useful introduction.

Mays, M. 'Inscriptions on British Celtic Coins', *Numismatic Chronicle* 152 (1992), 57–82.

Mays, M. (editor). *Celtic Coinage: Britain and Beyond.* British Archaeological Reports 222, 1992. Includes several valuable papers on the interpretation of coinage and on the technology of production.

Nash, D. *Coinage in the Celtic World.* Seaby, 1987. Concentrates on the social context of Celtic coinage throughout Europe.

Van Arsdell, R.D. *Celtic Coinage of Britain.* Spink, 1989. The fullest catalogue of British Celtic coinage.

Van Arsdell, R.D. *The Coinage of the Dobunni.* Oxford University Committee for Archaeology, 1994. A controversial interpretation of one tribe's coinage.

10
Museums

Although a number of museums hold significant collections of British Celtic coins, many do not have them on permanent display and it is advisable to contact the museum before visiting to check on their accessibility.

Ashmolean Museum of Art and Archaeology, Beaumont Street, Oxford OX1 2PH. Telephone: 01865 278000. Website: www.ashmol.ox.ac.uk

Birmingham Museum and Art Gallery, Chamberlain Square, Birmingham B3 3DH. Telephone: 0121 303 2834. Website: www.birmingham.gov.uk/bmag

British Museum, Great Russell Street, London WC1B 3DG. Telephone: 020 7636 1555. Website: www.thebritishmuseum.ac.uk

Fitzwilliam Museum, Trumpington Street, Cambridge CB2 1RB. Telephone: 01223 332900. Website: www.fitzmuseum.cam.ac.uk

Hunterian Museum and Art Gallery, University of Glasgow, Glasgow G12 8QQ. Telephone: 0141 330 4221. Website: www.gla.ac.uk/Museum

National Museum of Wales, Cathays Park, Cardiff CF10 3NP. Telephone: 029 20 397951. Website: www.nmgw.ac.uk

The Celtic Coin Index

The Celtic Coin Index is a collection of more than 31,000 records of Celtic coins found in Britain, incorporating a photograph and information on each coin. As such it is the largest and most important resource for all those researching aspects of British Celtic coinage. The success of the Celtic Coin Index is largely dependent on individual contributions, and readers who have information on Celtic coins or who have coins which they wish to be identified are encouraged to contact the Index at the Institute of Archaeology, 36 Beaumont Street, Oxford OX1 2PG (telephone: 01865 278240). Appointments to consult the Index can also be made by contacting this address, or through the Index website at: http://units.ox.ac.uk/departments/archaeology/ccindex/ccindex.htm.

Index